Stars
and
Galaxies

By James Buckley Jr.

Senior Editor Caryn Jenner
Assistant Editor Kritika Gupta
Art Editors Emma Hobson, Roohi Rais, Mohd. Zishan
Design Intern Sonali Mahthan
Jacket Co-ordinator Francesca Young
Jacket Designers Dheeraj Arora, Amy Keast
DTP Designers Vijay Kandwal, Dheeraj Singh
Picture Researcher Nishwan Rasool
Producer, Pre-Production Nadine King
Senior Producer Srijana Gurung
Deputy Managing Editor Vineetha Mokkil
Managing Editor Laura Gilbert
Managing Art Editors Neha Ahuja Chowdhry, Diane Peyton Jones
Art Director Martin Wilson
Publisher Sarah Larter

Educational consultant Jacqueline Harris

First published in Great Britain in 2017
by Dorling Kindersley Limited
80 Strand, London, WC2R 0RL

Copyright © 2017 Dorling Kindersley Limited
DK, a Penguin Random House Company
17 18 19 10 9 8 7 6 5 4 3 2 1
001—298636—April/17

A CIP catalogue record for this book is available from the British Library.

ISBN: 978-0-2412-8268-7

Printed and bound in China.

The publisher would like to thank the following for their kind permission to reproduce their photographs:
(Key: a-above; b-below/bottom; c-centre; f-far; l-left; r-right; t-top)

1 ESO: ESO / INAF-VST / OmegaCAM / A. Grado, L. Limatola / INAF-Capodimonte Observatory. 4-5 Getty Images:
Harpazo_Hope. 6-7 NASA: ESA / Hubble & NASA, Judy Schmidt. 8 Dreamstime.com: Lilkar. 9 Dreamstime.com: Lilkar. 10-11
ESA / Hubble: NASA, ESA, Harald Ebeling(University of Hawaii at Manoa) & Jean-Paul Kneib (LAM). 12-13 ESA / Hubble:
NASA (background). 15 Alamy Stock Photo: Angelina Stoykova. 16-17 Alamy Stock Photo: Angelina Stoykova. 18 ESA /
Hubble: NASA, ESA, N. Evans (Harvard-Smithsonian CfA), and H. Bond (STScI). 19 Alamy Stock Photo: Stocktrek Images, Inc.
(cb). 20-21 Alamy Stock Photo: Patrick Shyu. 22-23 ESA / Hubble: NASA. 24-25 ESA / Hubble: ESO. 26 NASA and The
Hubble Heritage Team (AURA/STScI): NASA, ESA, and the Hubble SM4 ERO Team. 28-29 ESO: ESO / José Francisco Salgado.
30-31 ESA / Hubble: NASA, ESA, G. Illingworth, D. Magee, and P. Oesch (University of California, Santa Cruz), R. Bouwens
(Leiden University), and the HUDF09 Team. 32 NASA: SDO (bl). 32-33 ESA / Hubble: NASA (background). NASA:
JPL-Caltech (br). 33 ESA / Hubble: NASA, ESA, G. Illingworth, D. Magee, and P. Oesch (University of California, Santa Cruz),
R. Bouwens (Leiden University), and the HUDF09 Team (cra). NASA: JPL-Caltech (cl). 34-35 123RF.com: Yuriy Mazur. 36
Dreamstime.com: Sissen2011 (bl). ESA / Hubble: NASA, ESA, and A. Dyer (background). 37 Dreamstime.com: Raphael Niederer
(t); Keren Segev (b). 38-39 NASA. 39 ESA / Hubble: NASA, ESA, and The Hubble Heritage Team (STScI / AURA) (b). NASA.
40-41 Alamy Stock Photo: B.A.E. Inc.. 42-43 ESA / Hubble: NASA (background). 44-45 ESA / Hubble: NASA (background)

Jacket images: *Front:* **Getty Images:** Marco Lorenzi, www.glitteringlights.com; *Back:* **Getty Images:** Christophe Lehenaff t;

Front Endpapers: **NASA:** X-ray: NASA / CXC / MSSL / R.Soria et al, Optical: AURA / Gemini OBs;
Back Endpapers: **NASA:** X-ray: NASA / CXC / MSSL / R.Soria et al, Optical: AURA / Gemini OBs

All other images © Dorling Kindersley
For further information see: www.dkimages.com

A WORLD OF IDEAS:
SEE ALL THERE IS TO KNOW
www.dk.com

Contents

Words in **bold** appear
in the glossary.

Chapter 1
Starlight

Stars fill the night sky with twinkling light. They make the night come alive!

Stars move around in space. They are far, far away from us. We see stars as tiny points of light.

Billions and billions of stars move through space. Stars look tiny because they're so far away. They're really huge balls of hot **gas**!

Far away in space, the stars glow brightly. This starlight takes many years to reach our planet, Earth.

Daytime

We can't see stars in the daytime because the Sun is too bright. The Sun is a star, too! It is the closest star to Earth.

Night time

The Sun gives Earth day and night, heat and light. Without the Sun, there would be no life on Earth.

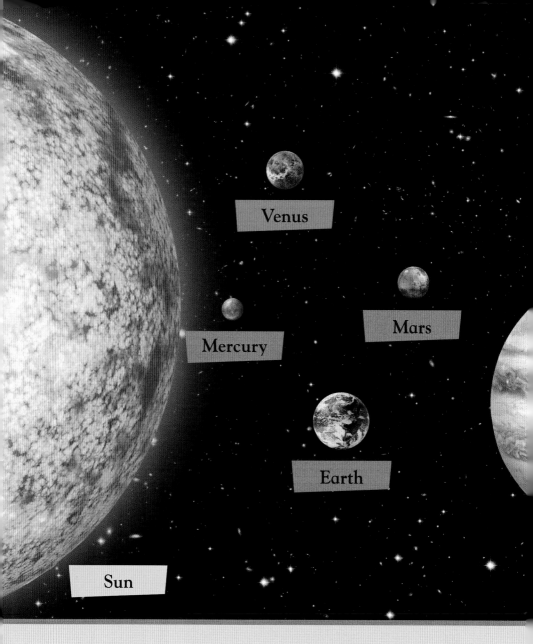

Venus

Mars

Mercury

Earth

Sun

Earth is one of eight planets that
orbit around the Sun. Other objects
in space also orbit around the Sun.

Saturn

Neptune

Uranus

Jupiter

The Sun, and everything that orbits around it, is called the **Solar System**.

Star Facts

★ Stars can be red, yellow, blue or white.

★ Stars come in many sizes, from a small **dwarf** to a huge **supergiant**!

★ The Sun is a yellow dwarf star. Imagine how big a supergiant star must be!

This red giant star is 25 times bigger than the Sun.

The Sun

This blue supergiant star is 75 times bigger than the Sun.

Chapter 2
Star Pictures

Long ago, people connected the "dots" of the stars to make pictures. They called these star pictures "constellations". Can you see a picture in the stars on the page opposite?

The constellation Orion

Orion the hunter

Connect the stars to meet Orion the hunter! The three bright stars in the middle make Orion's belt. Orion is a hunter in an ancient Greek **myth**.

North Star

Plough

There are many constellations in the sky. The Plough is a constellation that looks like a saucepan. The two stars at the end of the Plough point to the North Star. The North Star is very bright.

The Southern Cross is another constellation.

The North Star is always
in the same place in the sky.
Sailors can use the North Star
to help them work out which
direction they're going.

North Star

The Sky Zoo

Many constellations are pictures of animals. The constellations shown here are from a special group of constellations called the zodiac.

Cancer the crab

Leo the lion

Taurus the bull

Scorpio the scorpion

Capricorn the goat

Chapter 3
Groups of Stars

Stars gather in huge groups called galaxies. A galaxy is a group of billions of stars moving together in space.

Sometimes, groups of galaxies
move through space together.
That's a lot of stars!

Galaxies can be different shapes
and sizes. These are some common
galaxy shapes.

The Sun is a star in a galaxy called the Milky Way. From Earth, the Milky Way looks like a hazy white band across the night sky. A long time ago, people thought it looked like milk!

The **Universe** is truly enormous. It is filled with billions of galaxies. The galaxies are filled with billions of stars.

Our Place in Space

Earth may seem huge to you, but it is only a small part of space. So where exactly are we?

We are here! Planet Earth orbits the Sun, our special star.

The Sun is one of billions of stars in our galaxy.

Our galaxy is called
the Milky Way.

There are billions
of galaxies in
the Universe.

Chapter 4
Watching the Stars

If you want to watch the stars,
wait for a clear night when there
are no clouds.

Find a place far away from
the bright lights of towns
or cities.

Using a telescope or binoculars
will make the stars look closer.
Practice will make you a
real **stargazer**!

Telescope

Binoculars

These are some things that you might see in the night sky.

You might see a galaxy called Andromeda.

The moon is a big lump of rock among the stars. The moon orbits around Earth.

The Hubble Space Telescope orbits Earth. It takes amazing pictures from space, such as these far-off stars.

A scientist who studies the stars
and space is called an astronomer.

Now it's your turn to look up
at the night sky. What do you see?

Star Map

A star map can help you to
find stars and constellations
in the sky.

Stars and Galaxies Quiz

⭐ **1** What type of star is the Sun?

⭐ **2** What are star "pictures" called?

⭐ **3** What are huge groups of stars called?

⭐ **4** What is the name of the galaxy we live in?

⭐ **5** What does an astronomer study?

Answers on page 45.

Glossary

billions
a very large number,
more than 1,000,000,000

dwarf star
a star that is not as big or as bright
as a giant star or a supergiant star

gas
air-like substance that has no
fixed shape

myth
very old story known by
many people

orbit
to move around something
in space

stargazer
a person who likes to look
at or study stars

Solar System
the Sun, and the objects in space
that orbit around it, including
Earth and the other planets

supergiant star
largest and brightest type of star

Universe
everything that exists including
stars, planets and galaxies

Answers to Stars and Galaxies Quiz:

1. Yellow dwarf star; 2. Constellations;
3. Galaxies; 4. Milky Way; 5. The stars
and space

Guide for Parents

DK Readers is an exciting four-level reading series for children that will help to develop the habit of reading widely for both pleasure and information. These chapter books have an engaging main narrative to suit your child's reading ability, interspersed with additional information spreads in a range of reading genres. Each book is designed to develop your child's reading skills, fluency, grammar awareness, and comprehension in order to build confidence and pleasure in reading.

Ready for a *Beginning to Read* book

YOUR CHILD SHOULD

- be using phonics, including consonant blends, such as br, sp and st, to sound out unfamiliar words; and be familiar with common word endings, such as plurals, ing, ed and ly.

- be using the meaning of the text, the grammar of a sentence, plus clues from the illustrations to check and correct his/her own reading.

- be pausing briefly at commas, and for longer at full stops; and altering his/her expression for question, exclamation and speech marks.

A VALUABLE AND SHARED READING EXPERIENCE

For many children, reading requires a lot of effort, but adult participation can make this both fun and easier. So here are a few tips on how to use this book with your child.

TIP 1 **Check out the contents together before your child begins:**
- read the text about the book on the back cover.
- read through and discuss the contents page together to heighten your child's interest and expectation.
- have a brief discussion about unfamiliar or difficult words on each page.
- chat about the non-fiction reading features used in the book, such as headings, captions and labels.

TIP 2 Support your child as he/she reads each page:

- give the book to your child to read and turn the pages.

- where necessary, encourage your child to break a word into syllables, sound out each one, and then flow the syllables together. Ask him/her to reread the sentence to check the meaning.

- you may need to help read some topic-related vocabulary and other words that may be difficult for your child.

- when there's a question mark or an exclamation mark, encourage your child to vary his/her voice as he/she reads the sentence. Demonstrate how to do this if it is helpful.

TIP 3 Praise, share and chat:

- the additional information spreads are designed to be shared and discussed with your child. These spreads tend to be more difficult than the main narrative.

- ask your child questions about the meaning of the text and of the words used. This will help to develop comprehension skills and awareness of the language used.

A FEW ADDITIONAL TIPS

- Encourage your child to try reading difficult words by themselves. Praise any self-corrections, for example, "I like the way you sounded out that word and then changed the way you said it to make sense."

- Try to read together every day. Reading little and often is best. These books are divided into manageable chapters for one reading session. However, after 10 minutes, only keep going if your child wants to read on.

- Read a variety of books of different types with your child for pleasure and information. Reading aloud to your child is a great way to develop his or her reading skills!

- Make reading an enjoyable experience for your child.

Index